A History of Music

LAKE PARK HIGH SCHOOL
ROSELLE, IL 60172

ESSENTIAL LIBRARY OF CULTURAL HISTORY

A HISTORY OF *Music*

by Shannon Baker Moore

Content Consultant
Barry T. Bilderback, PhD
University of Idaho/Lionel Hampton School of Music

An Imprint of Abdo Publishing | www.abdopublishing.com

www.abdopublishing.com

Published by Abdo Publishing, a division of ABDO, PO Box 398166, Minneapolis, Minnesota 55439. Copyright © 2015 by Abdo Consulting Group, Inc. International copyrights reserved in all countries. No part of this book may be reproduced in any form without written permission from the publisher. Essential Library™ is a trademark and logo of Abdo Publishing.

Printed in the United States of America, North Mankato, Minnesota
102014
012015

THIS BOOK CONTAINS RECYCLED MATERIALS

Cover Photo: Valentin Agapov/Shutterstock Images
Interior Photos: Mario Cales/Shutterstock Images, 1 (left), 51; Library of Congress, 1 (right), 82, 89; Denis Kuvaev/Shutterstock Images, 3 (top), 33; AP Images, 3 (bottom), 85, 93, 101; Bettmann/Corbis, 7, 40, 66, 68; Stuart Monk/Shutterstock Images, 11; Shutterstock Images, 13, 23, 75; Daniel Maurer/AP Images, 14; Gerard van Honthorst, 25; Public Domain, 27, 61 (top), 98; François Morellon de La Cave, 37; Richard Lewis/AP Images, 44; Giovanni Paolo Panini, 49; Alfredo Dagli Orti/The Art Archive/Corbis, 55, 63; Louis Carrogis Carmontelle, 57; Thomas Hardy, 60, 99; Karl Joseph Stieler, 61 (bottom), 100; Bain Collection/Library of Congress, 78; Universal Attractions, 90; Suzy Patterson/AP Images, 96

Editor: Jenna Gleisner
Series Designer: Maggie Villaume

Library of Congress Control Number: 2014943864

Cataloging-in-Publication Data

Moore, Shannon Baker.
 A history of music / Shannon Baker Moore.
  p. cm. -- (Essential library of cultural history)
 ISBN 978-1-62403-555-5 (lib. bdg.)
 Includes bibliographical references and index.
 1. Sound recordings--History--Juvenile literature. 2. Music--History--Juvenile literature. I. Title.
 780--dc23

2014943864

CONTENTS

Chapter 1
THE EXPLOSION OF MUSIC   6

Chapter 2
ANCIENT INFLUENCES   12

Chapter 3
THE RISE OF THE RENAISSANCE   24

Chapter 4
SPECTACULAR SOUNDS   36

Chapter 5
A SHIFT TO LIGHTER MUSIC   50

Chapter 6
ROMANTIC PIANISTS   62

Chapter 7
A TIME OF CHANGE   74

Chapter 8
THE RISE OF ROCK 'N' ROLL   88

Timeline	98	Source Notes	106
Glossary	102	Index	110
Additional Resources	104	About the Author	112

Chapter 1

The Explosion of Music

On January 13, 1910, legendary vocalist Enrico Caruso, known as the Great Caruso, was scheduled to sing at the Metropolitan Opera in New York. Sitting in the lush red and gold colors of the opera house, the audience buzzed with excitement to hear him sing. Lee de Forest, one of the early pioneers of radio, was even more excited. He wanted to record Caruso on the radio. De Forest's radio transmitter was set and ready to go. Then the curtain rose, de Forest hit a switch, and history was made. It was the first public radio broadcast in history. Although there were no private radios in US homes at the time, several locations in New York City set up public receivers. Those interested could put

Famous opera singer Enrico Caruso performed at the Metropolitan Opera more than 600 times.

THE POWER OF THE MICROPHONE

For much of human history, vocal music was only as loud as the singer. Singers had to project their voices, singing loudly and clearly enough to be heard over an orchestra in a large concert hall full of people. This singing required special training to maximize volume and projection. With the invention of the microphone in 1876, it became possible to project a voice electronically. Vocal training was no longer essential in order to be heard. The microphone could project lighter, more natural voices.

on earphones at these locations and hear Caruso sing.

Caruso was an international celebrity, a musical superstar whose success outshined all other singers in his lifetime. Caruso was also an early fan of technology. One of the first musicians to record his music, Caruso recorded his song "Vesti la Giubba" in 1902 for the phonograph. Caruso's song sold more than 1 million copies, the first recording to do so.[1]

Music is often taken for granted today. It is everywhere—in the grocery store, on our car radios, in movies and television shows, and on our computers, phones, and MP3 players. With a click or the touch of a button, we can now hear whatever we want—an entire orchestra, a rock concert with pounding bass, or a new song written by an undiscovered artist on the other side of the world.

However, for most of human history, music has not been so readily available. In the past, music was not recorded or written. Once it was written, few people had access to printed music. Also, few people owned instruments. The very first instrument was the human voice, and the very first music was passed from person to person by memory.

Music in Western Civilization

Music spans all cultures and stems from humankind's earliest beginnings. It is a global phenomenon most likely far older than recorded history. And music continues to evolve. Western music focuses on music with roots in Europe and European-influenced countries around the world, such as the United States. Western music began in the ancient cultures of the Mediterranean, including ancient Greece and Rome, and then spread

Background Music

Within many public places, such as malls, dentist offices, elevators, and restaurants, music can be heard. This background music, also called ambient music, is a relatively recent phenomenon. In the 1920s, George Squier realized music could influence customers and employees. For example, soft arrangements of well-known songs could make customers stay in stores longer. Squier founded Muzak, a company that sold specially programmed music to businesses. By 2000, ambient music was the most common kind of music heard worldwide. Nicknamed elevator music, ambient music is heard by more than 100 million listeners each day.[2]

throughout Europe and the globe. Today, Western music provides a common musical language used by cultures worldwide. In turn, Western music also borrows from music cultures throughout the world. Now more than ever, technology connects music cultures everywhere.

The history of Western music is often told as periods of successive art movements. In music, however, dates and definitions for these artistic periods differ a bit from other kinds of art, such as literature, painting, and architecture. The history of music shows some current and common musical elements, such as rhythm and beat, were not always a part of Western music, or were different or not accounted for. Other elements that seem modern and innovative may in fact be simply a new twist on an old tradition. Cultures from around the world have similar patterns in their music.

All known cultures, both ancient and modern, have created music, and music is a way to express some of our deepest emotions. Music has many functions and is found in most public activities and rituals: military marches, national anthems, graduation ceremonies, and religious festivals. Music is also incorporated into the most private moments: lullabies, love songs, and tunes in the shower. Music is part of the human identity, who we

Music is incorporated in many facets of our lives, including public festivities such as parades.

are and what we value. Millions loved the Great Caruso, not because they understood or even enjoyed opera, but because they were moved by the powerful emotions in his velvety voice.

Chapter 2

Ancient Influences

Music seems to have existed since the human species began. The oldest paintings on cave walls date from 32,000 BCE. Even older ancient instruments exist. Very little is known about ancient music from prehistoric times before people kept written records. Even after record keeping began, the history of music is difficult to trace because music was largely an oral tradition passed from one person to another by voice and instrument. Most cultures had no methods of music notation, or ways of writing music. As a result, music historians do not know how music sounded in ancient cultures. Nevertheless, records and artifacts provide some clues about how Western music developed.

In ancient civilizations such as Greece, people believed their gods created music and instruments.

The oldest known instruments were flutes discovered in Germany that date from 43,000 to 42,000 BCE.

Ancient Egyptian tombs contain visual images, such as paintings and carvings, depicting musical instruments including horns, flutes, harps, and percussion instruments. In 1939, two trumpets unearthed from King Tut's tomb were actually played during a radio broadcast. An ancient Babylonian clay tablet, dating from 2000 to 1700 BCE, is the oldest example of understandable written music. This tablet included some instructions for playing notes on a four-string lute. Other fragments of notated music have survived from ancient Greece. Some of the oldest existing song lyrics are the Psalms of David from the Old Testament of the Bible. Their ancient tunes are unknown, so these psalms are often open to interpretation and sung to different music.

Music in Ancient Greece

Greece is the ancient civilization with the most influence on Western music. In Greek mythology, the gods invented music and were the first musicians. The ancient Greeks believed nine Muses, or goddesses, inspired art and science. In fact, the word *music* comes from the Greek word *mousike*, meaning "an art or science directed by the muses."

Ancient Greeks believed music and poetry were inseparable. Music, an essential part of Greek culture and rituals, was included in the Olympics Games. These games were both athletic and religious festivals. Greeks also created singing competitions in which participants sang for a live audience and panel of judges.

Music was an important part of Greek education as well. To the ancient Greeks, studying music

ANCIENT ORGANS

The ancient Greeks invented the organ. This organ used water to pressurize air for the organ pipes. In 1931, archaeologists found an ancient Roman hydraulis organ. Built in 228 BCE, this organ belonged to a company of Roman firefighters. Organs were a popular Roman instrument. The organ was played during shows of public entertainment, such as gladiator competitions. Today, organs are still used for public sporting events, such as baseball games.

> The world's oldest playable organ was built between 1390 and 1435 CE, 150 years before the first pencil.

helped educate people and build good character. Because music was viewed as an art and a science, Greek music theory connected to astronomy and math. Ancient Greeks believed there was a celestial music. This "music of the spheres" kept planets and stars in their proper orbit.

Greek philosopher and mathematician Pythagoras (570 BCE–500 BCE) is said to have discovered the relationship between music and math. According to legend, Pythagoras discovered the relationship between musical sound and math while walking past a blacksmith's shop. As he heard the sound of the blacksmith's hammer, Pythagoras noticed different weighted hammers created different pitches. For example, if one hammer weighed ten pounds (4.5 kg) and another weighed five pounds (2.3 kg), this would create a ratio of 2:1, and the two hammers would sound an octave apart. An octave is an interval of eight notes, including the bottom and top notes. Pythagoras discovered that a ratio of 3:2 created sounds that were a fifth, or five notes, apart. Pythagoras's discovery greatly influenced Western music theory.

Another important musical contribution from ancient Greece is drama. In Greek tradition, drama combined musical, literary, and staged arts—the ancestor of today's musical. All Greek drama had music and singers who were referred to collectively as the chorus. The chorus sang lines about the action happening onstage. Although Greek drama is very different from a Broadway musical, the roots of Broadway are in ancient Greece.

The Medieval Period

The Romans conquered ancient Greece in 146 BCE. The Roman Empire spread throughout Europe and the Mediterranean. Eventually, the Roman Empire split in two. In the western region, Christianity became dominant as both a religion and ruling force. This period, which began around 400 CE,

MEDIEVAL COMPOSER HILDEGARD OF BINGEN
Hildegard of Bingen was one of the most extraordinary composers of the medieval period. She was known as a leader, composer, poet, diplomat, and prophet. Hildegard grew up in a German monastery and eventually became its leader, an abbess. Hildegard later founded two other monasteries. Considering she lived during a time when women were not allowed to go to school or become church leaders, Hildegard's accomplishments were truly remarkable. She wrote two large collections of church music, including a sacred musical drama featuring 82 songs.

is called the Middle Ages, or the medieval period. The medieval period covers almost 1,000 years of history. Of course, one musical period does not stop suddenly as another begins. Changes happen gradually with time.

As in ancient Greece and Rome, players memorized music during medieval times. The practice of notation did not become widespread until approximately 900 CE. Early medieval music was the music of early Christianity, and it took the form of chanting. Called plainchant or plainsong, chanting is a practice some scholars think was passed down from the Hebrew chants of ancient Israel. Plainchant is also sometimes called Gregorian chant after Pope Gregory I. For the first half of this era, plainchant was the main type of music heard in the church.

> **Fantasy movies such as the Lord of the Rings series or films set in medieval times often use actual songs from the medieval period.**

Plainchant was sung a cappella, without instrumental accompaniment. The chant was also monophonic, so everyone sang the exact same notes. Because of the widespread belief that the Christian Holy Spirit directly delivered plainchant to the pope, plainchant remained the same for hundreds of years.

The first change to plainchant was singing the same notes but with one part higher or lower than the other. Imagine a group of priests singing with a choir of young boys. The priests and the boys sang the same notes, but the men's voices were much lower than the boys'. In the musical scale of do-re-mi-fa-sol-la-ti-do, the men sang the low *do* and the boys sang the high *do*.

Hundreds of years later, the next big change came. What if instead of just singing the low *do* and the high *do*, the choir combined a *do* with a *fa*? This would create harmony—notes that complement each other but are not the same pitch. With time, more changes were introduced into religious music, including polyphony, meaning many voices or pitches. Polyphonic music has two or more melodies of equal importance that are sung together.

PLAINCHANT AND POPE GREGORY I

Medieval people believed plainchant was a holy gift from God. Illustrated medieval manuscripts show Pope Gregory I with a bird sitting on his shoulder. The bird is said to be the Holy Spirit in the form of a dove dictating the chants into the pope's ear. The illustrations also show a scribe peeking from behind a screen to see Gregory receiving the chants. Although some medieval people thought Gregory I composed all the chants himself, plainchant existed before Pope Gregory I but was not written down until 200 years after his papacy.

Most medieval music grew from existing melodies. Monks added to existing chants by using tropes. The term *trope* comes from the Latin word *tropus*, which means "a turn of phrase." In music, a trope is an addition that fancies up a simpler musical phrase. Tropes could be added to any part of a chant—beginning, middle, or end. The original chant was still there but with some additional material.

Music Notation

Until the Middle Ages, there was no standard system for writing down music. Singers memorized their music, and there were hundreds of different tunes used in the various church services throughout the

Medieval Instruments

Medieval instruments differed from today's instruments and had different names. For example, the medieval trombone was called a sackbut. Medieval instruments were earlier versions of modern instruments such as recorders, flutes, guitars, violins, and trombones. The vielle was an ancestor of the violin. The rebec was a small pear-shaped instrument with three to five strings. The shawm was a popular wind instrument. During the medieval period, instrumental and vocal music were somewhat interchangeable. One instrument could be substituted for another. A singer may have filled in for an instrument. People made music with whatever instruments and musicians they had.

year. In an effort to help his choir learn music more easily, the monk Guido of Arezzo recommended a new method in the 1000s. He suggested arranging notes on lines—and on the spaces in between—to show how the notes related to one another. Guido of Arezzo's method worked. Suddenly musicians had music they could read. No longer did they have to sing only from memory.

> **The well-known medieval song "Chanson de Roland" ("Song of Roland"), is more than 4,000 lines long.**

Notation forever changed the history of music. Some argue it was as important to Western music as writing was to literature and language.

Despite the new developments with notation, written music still did not have a way to show rhythm. Characters to indicate long notes, short notes, and pauses did not yet exist. A consistent system for noting rhythm patterns would not emerge until approximately 1280 CE.

John Dunstable and the Third

Another musical change of enormous importance was the growth of a chord combination known as a third. A chord is two or more notes played at the same time. Originally, plainchant was monophonic, so it had no chords. However, when plainchant began including polyphony, plainchant used chords. Plainchant used chord combinations favored by Pythagoras. These chord combinations were the octave (eight notes apart), the fourth (four notes apart), and the fifth (five notes apart).

In the early 1400s, English composer John Dunstable started using a new chord combination—the third. The notes *do* and *mi* are a third. Today, this chord combination is commonplace. But in Dunstable's day, thirds were revolutionary, and his fame spread as people fell in love with this captivating new sound. Dunstable also used groups of thirds to build another powerful chord combination called the triad. Triads are the chords around which Western music is constructed. The medieval music known today, including Dunstable's thirds, survived primarily because it was written down by priests who could read and write.

Piano Keyboard

The white keys on a piano keyboard range from C, D, E, F, G, A, B, and back to C. Each set is known as an octave. There are seven octaves on a standard piano. The black keys on the keyboard serve as sharp (♯) and flat (♭) notes for each white key. Sharps indicate a slight increase in pitch. Flats decrease the pitch of a note. A third is an interval of three notes.

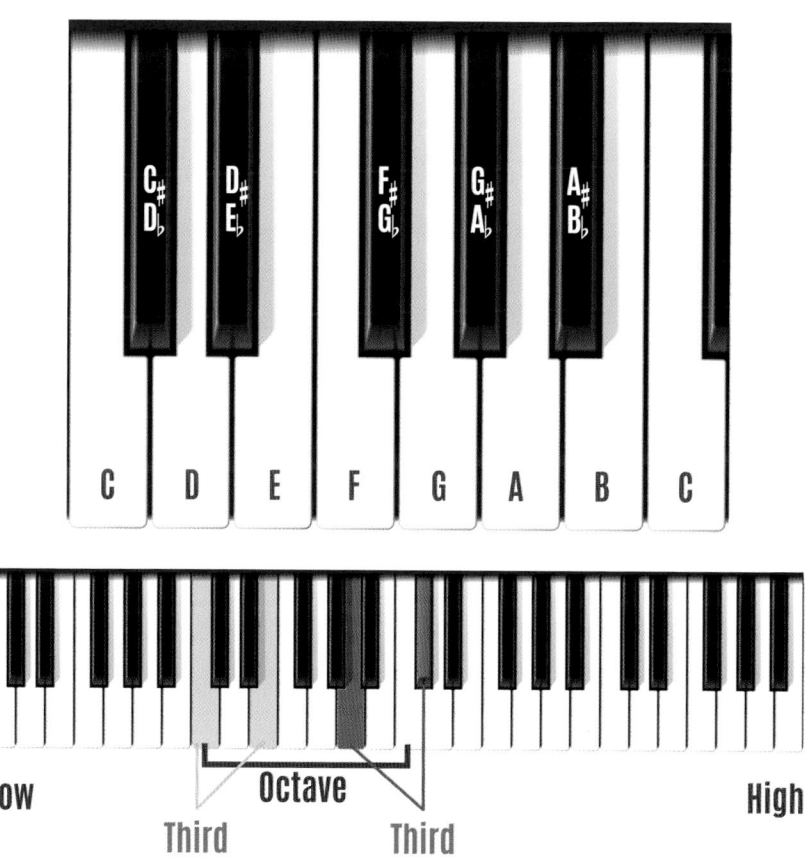

Chapter 3

The Rise of the Renaissance

In 1453, Turks invaded the city of Constantinople, which is now called Istanbul, Turkey. Many scholars fled to the West, bringing ancient manuscripts with them. The recovery of these works sparked a new interest in the civilizations of Greece and Rome. This rediscovery of ancient learning, along with new discoveries and inventions, produced the era known as the Renaissance, or "rebirth," around the 1400s to 1600s. Italy was home to many famous Renaissance artists, including Michelangelo and Leonardo da Vinci. But many of the Renaissance composers and musicians who are best known today came from Northern Europe rather than Italy.

String-instrument playing improved during the Renaissance with the introduction of the bow.

Music and the Nobility

During the Renaissance, ancient Greek views about music shaped European ideas. It was understood music had the power to influence character and emotion. Music was part of a refined person's education as well. The ability to sing, play, and read music were essential skills for a refined person. Even Henry VIII (1491–1547), king of England, was proud of his skill as composer and singer. His daughter, Elizabeth I (1533–1603), was also an accomplished lute and keyboard player.

Similar to fine clothes and castles, music was a status symbol. Nobility competed to employ the best musicians and composers. It was also fashionable for aristocrats to have their own chapel complete with a church composer and musicians at their court. A typical aristocrat supported between 12 and 20 musicians.[1] Court musicians often worked at multiple courts throughout

QUEEN ELIZABETH I AS MUSICIAN

British King Henry VIII and his second wife, Anne Boleyn, composed and performed music. Their daughter, Elizabeth, later crowned Queen Elizabeth I, was known as an accomplished lute and keyboard player. In one painting of Elizabeth as queen, she is shown holding a lute. A nobleman wrote that Elizabeth played "excellently well."[2]

Music for "Pastime with Good Company," composed by King Henry VIII

their lives. As musicians traveled throughout Europe, they adopted musical techniques from other regions. During the Renaissance, a more international style of music arose, combining styles from England, France, and Italy.

Features of Renaissance Music

As part of their admiration for Greek art, Renaissance musicians sought to create beautiful and orderly music. Renaissance polyphony, also known as counterpoint, emphasized sweet sounding music and pleasing tones. Renaissance composers wanted their music to be consonant. Consonant music notes sound nice together,

HOLDING THE LINE

Barbershop music is a type of music that still has a lower voice carrying the melody. In a barbershop quartet, the melody is sung by the second-highest voice. The highest voice and the two lowest voices support the main melody. Barbershop quartets get their name from the barbershops of the 1500 and 1600s. While customers waited, instead of reading magazines or watching television, they could play instruments that were available. The barbershop music of today is a singing style with four-part harmony, which developed in the United States in the late 1800s.

not jarring or inharmonious. Music that sounds happy or peaceful is usually consonant. Dissonant music is music that sounds sad or scary. Medieval plainchant sometimes sounds dissonant.

Another difference between medieval and Renaissance music was melody. In the Middle Ages, musicians assumed the melody, or main tune, was sung by the lower voices and the higher voices accompanied, or supported, the lower ones. The male vocal part tenor comes from the French verb *tenir*, meaning "to hold," because the tenor part held, or contained, the melody in the Middle Ages. In medieval music, lower voices were the main ingredient. Higher voices were like seasoning. With time, however, the melody began moving higher. By approximately 1500 CE, the highest voices usually sang the melody.

Paraphrasing was a popular technique composers used during the Renaissance. In music, paraphrasing means taking an existing melody and rewriting it. Composers made the music their own by changing the rhythm and adding or changing notes.

Josquin des Prez's Word Painting

Most of the Renaissance composers known today began as choirboys who grew up singing and then composed for church or court chapels. The most admired composer of the era was Josquin des Prez. Most likely born in northern France, des Prez worked for nobility in France and Italy, then later for the church in France. Other musicians of his day called him the best composer of the time. Some compared him to Michelangelo—an artist without an equal in music. His religious composition "Ave Maria . . . virgo serena" has been called the Mona Lisa of Renaissance music.

Des Prez was best known for his ability to create music that reflected and enhanced the meaning of the words. His music added emotion to the text of the church mass. Today the connection

> **During the Renaissance, a Spanish stringed instrument similar to a lute called a vilhuela could have as many as 35 strings.[3]**

between music and emotion seems obvious. However, during the medieval period this connection was not often made. The connection was obvious to the ancient Greeks, however, and Renaissance music revived this classical idea.

One way des Prez created emotion was through a method called word painting. Word painting uses music to create or paint an image of the words being sung. For example, if the words of the song are about a hopping frog, the music jumps from low notes to high notes to imitate a frog.

Before the Renaissance, notated music had all been handwritten. When Johannes Gutenberg invented the moveable-type printing press in 1450, printing music became possible as well. Italian printer Ottaviano Petrucci published the first book of printed music in 1501. Des Prez's music was so popular Petrucci published three volumes of des Prez's work. Petrucci usually printed only one volume per composer.

With printing, music was suddenly much easier to produce and much more affordable. Notated music was no longer for professional musicians and the nobility only. Even amateurs could afford music. The increased demand for music led to new kinds of songs and much more instrumental music. Dance music was also popular, for both stately, formal occasions and folk dances. More music also meant a boom in solo musical performances. The Renaissance emphasized the importance of the individual. Composers often deliberately wrote music that was difficult to play to show off a composer or musician's talent.

Renaissance Instruments

As instruments became more available, they also began to change during the Renaissance. Popular stringed instruments, such as the vilhuela and the lute, had been plucked by hand or with a small pick called a plectrum. However, in the late 1400s, musicians began using a bow strung with horsehair. By 1500, the instrument families of wind, percussion, and strings were

The Challenge of Printing Music

Printing music was different from printing text because printed music was composed of lines, music notes, and words. Petrucci printed each sheet of music three times. The first time he printed the lines of the staff onto the paper. For the second printing, he added words onto the paper. During the final print run, Petrucci added the notes. In the 1520s, printers in London, England, and Paris, France, started using a system that printed lines, notes, and words all at once. It was quicker and less expensive, but it did not look quite as smooth and polished as Petrucci's method.

well established. Violin-like instruments developed into the more modern violin near the early 1500s.

The making of a beautiful instrument was an art and a closely guarded secret. What wood to use, how thick to cut it, how to shape it, how to varnish it—all of these details and more went into the crafting of an instrument. Andrea Amati built the oldest surviving violin in 1564. Amati's grandson Niccoli had two outstanding apprentices. Both opened their own shops and founded two of the most famous violin-making families in history: the Stradivari and the Guarneri. Violins made by the legendary Antonio Stradivari of the late 1600s and early 1700s are still prized today and are used by some of the world's best musicians.

The Protestant Reformation

During the Renaissance, people challenged traditions as well as music. Before the 1500s, Western Europe had only one church: the Catholic Church. Worship services were spoken and sung in Latin. The church obeyed the pope, the head of the Catholic Church. Then in 1517, German monk and Catholic priest Martin Luther

Violins made by Andrea and Niccoli Amati and Antonio Stradivari are on display at the Cité de la Musique Museum in Paris, France.

LOVE SONGS

Similar to today, love songs were popular during the Renaissance. One of the most famous books of Renaissance love songs is the *Chansonnier Cordiforme*. *Chanson* is French for "song." The *Chansonnier Cordiforme* manuscript is shaped like a heart. When opened, it looks like a double heart with music for love songs written inside. The music is decorated with beautiful artwork along the edges.

challenged the established order by protesting some of the Catholic practices of the time. The Protestant Reformation, as it was called, ended religious unity in Europe. New kinds of religious music arose as new religions appeared. In Catholic services, only the church choir sang. Martin Luther believed music could bring people closer to God. Luther enjoyed choirs, but he also wanted church members to sing in church.

Because Luther was also a composer, he wrote music that was easy for a church congregation to sing. Luther's composition "A Mighty Fortress Is Our God" is still sung in churches today. Luther also wrote new words for folk tunes, and these became hymns for church services. So more worshipers would understand the messages, churches also began holding services in the local language, for example German or English, rather than only in Latin.

The Catholic Church responded by adding more congregational singing to their services as well. Sacred music moved away from complicated polyphony sung by trained choirs. To more clearly convey the message of the words, new church music was simpler, with a melody, accompanying chords, and a supporting bass line. This type of music is called homophony—music in which one melody line is supported by chords or other musical material—and is still heard in pop music today. Some composers wanted to keep both the old polyphony and the new homophony. They wrote music that switched between the two, and this became known as High Renaissance Style. As with other cultural arts, music blossomed during the Renaissance. As instruments and printed music became more widely available, performances increased and more musical variety developed.

Chapter 4

Spectacular Sounds

The word *baroque* comes from the Portuguese word *barroco*, a term used to describe a misshapen pearl with an exaggerated or abnormal shape. The term *baroque* was originally used by critics in the 1700s because they thought baroque music was too exaggerated and ornate. It was not natural and simple like a round, normal pearl.

Baroque music has a number of characteristics that set it apart from Renaissance music. Renaissance music focused on pleasing, consonant sounds. Thanks to the inspiration of composer Claudio Monteverdi and his madrigals—nonreligious music that led to the singing style heard in opera—baroque musicians, on the other hand, wanted music to sound more dramatic and

Antonio Vivaldi is often regarded as one of the greatest baroque composers.

spectacular. They wanted music to stir the emotions of listeners. Baroque composers were willing to break musical rules for emotional effect. They experimented with more daring combinations of notes and more dissonance. Music also became more ornamented. Features such as trills and fancy solos let musicians change the music to make it more dramatic.

The baroque musicians Johann Sebastian Bach and George Frideric Handel were both born in 1685 in Germany. Although they are both revered as two of the most famous baroque composers, the two never met, and their careers took very different directions.

THE MUSICAL BACH FAMILY

Johann Sebastian Bach came from a remarkably musical family. More than 70 of his family members were professional musicians.[1] Today, Johann Sebastian Bach is the most famous musician in the Bach family, but this was not always the case. Bach had two sons, Carl Philipp Emanuel and Johann Christian, and their reputation was greater than their father's in the late 1700s. The two were half brothers, sons of Johann Sebastian Bach's first and second wives.

Johann Sebastian Bach

Johann Sebastian Bach's father had been an organist and town musician, and Bach followed in his father's footsteps. He took both organ and harpsichord lessons. By age 15, Bach was a church chorister, and at age 18 he got his first job as an organist. A devout Lutheran, Bach believed music should glorify God. Bach was a masterful musician of unusual skill and talent.

Nevertheless, having never traveled extensively, Bach's music was not well-known outside his own country of Germany during his lifetime. Fewer than 12 of his compositions were printed before his death. He did not make a lot of money from his music either, and Bach's widow died in poverty. Many considered his music old-fashioned. Bach did not become famous until 1828, when renowned composer Felix Mendelssohn rediscovered and conducted Bach's *St. Matthew Passion* oratorio.

Romantic composer Richard Wagner said *St. Matthew Passion* is "the most stupendous miracle in all music."[2] Today Bach is considered one of the greatest composers in Western music. Because he learned to compose by copying and arranging music from many countries, his music blended styles in new ways. Some even say he was better at composing in French and Italian styles than the French and Italian composers themselves. His highest achievement was his use of relating and staggering melodies in his style of polyphony, also called counterpoint. Bach's

J. S. Bach's Famous Oratorio

Bach's *St. Matthew Passion* was first performed on Good Friday in 1727. Composed for Holy Week, the week leading up to the Christian celebration of Easter, the piece tells the story of the crucifixion of Jesus Christ. *St. Matthew Passion* is an oratorio, a religious version of an opera. An oratorio has a narrator, characters, and a chorus, but unlike opera, it does not usually have costumes, sets, or stage action.

St. Matthew Passion contains 68 sections that take more than three hours to perform. A tenor sings as narrator, a soloist plays the part of Jesus and other important characters, and a choir sings the words of Jesus's followers, the crowd, and other groups. At times, the choir is similar to a chorus in a Greek drama commenting on events. According to composer Howard Goodall, *St. Matthew Passion* is "one of the crowning creative achievements in all European culture."[3]

One example of its dramatic beauty is the opening chorus. Bach used a double-sized orchestra and two adult choirs for maximum effect. Then he layered a slower melody on top, a children's choir singing "O innocent lamb of God." The effect is incredibly dramatic and moving.

music is rich, dramatic, and powerful. His religious music is particularly moving.

George Frideric Handel

Baroque composer George Frideric Handel, on the other hand, traveled and had an international reputation during his lifetime. Handel's father did not want his son to pursue music as a career. As a result, although his father permitted organ lessons, he studied law at a university. He did not become a full-time musician until after his father's death.

At age 18, Handel got a job as a violinist in a German opera house. Then at age 21, Handel moved to Italy, the center of Western music. Like Hollywood for movies or Nashville, Tennessee, for country music, Italy was the place to be for composers in the 1700s. In Italy, Handel met prominent musicians and composers and mastered their styles. He caught on quickly—in fact, he was proclaimed a genius. After a

BACH AND THE FUGUE
Bach is well known for a type of music called a fugue. *Fugue* is Italian for "flight." A fugue is similar to a very complex round. Once when Bach was at court, the king's musicians composed a tune they thought would never work as a fugue. It would be horribly dissonant. Fugues were out of style anyway. Nevertheless, Bach sat at the keyboard and instantly improvised a lovely three-part fugue based on the tune. Everyone was amazed. Later Bach sent the king a six-part fugue composed from the same tune.

successful Italian opera and a short return to Germany, Handel settled in London.

Handel worked as a composer. In 1727, he composed "Zadok the Priest" for the coronation of Britain's King George III. This composition has been performed at every British coronation ceremony since. Handel's public rehearsal of his *Music for the Royal Fireworks* attracted 12,000 people and stopped traffic for three hours. Handel's *Messiah*, with its rousing "Hallelujah" chorus, is his most famous work. During his lifetime, Handel gained international fame. His music has been regularly performed ever since. Many musicians and composers are like stars that burn brightly and then die out. But Handel is the first composer whose music has never stopped being performed.

Like Bach, Handel was influenced by many national styles of music. As one of the greatest composers of his time, Handel mastered all types of vocal and instrumental music. In addition to his Italian operas, his most important contribution was his development of sacred opera—the dramatic oratorio. Handel wrote many oratorios in addition to his famous *Messiah*.

Other European Composers

Of course, Bach and Handel were not the only prominent composers of their day. Bach worked in Germany, and Handel worked in England. Meanwhile in France, Jean-Baptiste Lully (1632–1687) wrote elaborate operas and ballets for King Louis XIV. Italian-born Lully (his real name was Giovanni Battista Lulli) was the son of a poor miller and arrived in France at age 14. His singing talent earned him a job as an apprentice in the court of Louis XIV. He then worked his way up to ballet dancer, superintendent of music at court, and finally music master to the royal family itself. King Louis XIV himself performed in some of Lully's ballets.

One of Lully's innovations was adding wind, brass, and percussion instruments to the king's string orchestra. Louis XIV used a 24-instrument violin ensemble, but he also had a 40-instrument ensemble called the *Grand Ecurie* (French for "great stable").[4] This wind, brass, and percussion band was used for outdoor

THE KING STANDS FOR HANDEL

Today, Handel's most famous work is *Messiah*, particularly its "Hallelujah" chorus. In 1743, King George II attended a performance and was so moved by the chorus that he stood up. When the king stood, everyone else stood as well. The tradition is still carried on today. Modern audiences attending a performance of Handel's *Messiah* stand for the "Hallelujah" chorus.

The Handel House Museum in London, former home of Handel, houses a portrait of Handel as well as a harpsichord similar to the ones Handel played.

performances and military events. Lully brought the two groups together for some performances.

In Italy, the violinist-composer Arcangelo Corelli, a virtuoso, was experimenting with violin music. Corelli pioneered modern bowing techniques for the violin. He played so passionately his face would become contorted and his eyes would redden and "roll as if in agony."[5] Corelli (1653–1713) was also deeply interested in conveying emotion through dynamics—how loudly or softly music is played.

> In September 1581, a ballet was staged as part of the royal wedding festivities for King Henry II of France and Catherine de Medici. The performance began at 10:00 p.m. and did not end until 3:00 a.m.

At the time, many instruments were not designed to gradually sound louder or softer. For example, musical notes played at the same volume whether a musician pressed gently or pounded on a harpsichord key. Corelli compensated for this problem by having an ensemble of many players. Sometimes the whole group, such as all string instruments, would play, whereas at other times only a few musicians would play. In this way, the dynamics and the mood of the piece could be better controlled. Corelli also helped develop the concerto, a musical

VIVALDI

In his four violin concertos known as *The Four Seasons*, Vivaldi uses music to depict spring, summer, autumn, and winter. Vivaldi creates the sound of melting snow dripping by plucking high notes on the violin. He depicts chattering teeth with violins playing repeated notes at a furious speed. Through music, Vivaldi creates pictures in his listeners' minds. In his music, listeners hear everything from birds and mosquitoes to storms and rivers.

form that features a solo instrument in the lead role with other instruments accompanying.

During the baroque period, concertos were very popular. One famous violinist-composer, Antonio Vivaldi, wrote more than 500 concertos. Vivaldi's concertos *The Four Seasons* are probably his best-known works.

Another important development during the baroque era was that instrument tuning became more consistent and standardized. Tuning prepares an instrument so it will sound at the correct pitch. If instruments are not tuned before a performance, notes can be slightly off pitch. One instrument may play slightly too high and another slightly too low.

In the 1500s, there were several different tuning systems, depending on the instrument. Lutists used one tuning system. Keyboardists used another. Violinists used still another. These different tuning systems made it challenging to play together. Eventually tuning became more standardized. During the baroque period, instruments began to consistently use tuning called equal temperament. Instruments that previously had not worked well together could now play more easily together.

The harpsichord had been a popular keyboard instrument, but another exciting new keyboard was gaining popularity: the piano. The piano was originally invented in approximately 1700 CE by Italian instrument-maker Bartolomeo Cristofori. It was called *piano e il forte*, Italian for "soft and loud." Although Cristofori's invention was not very popular in Italy, German organ maker Gottfried Silbermann also started building pianos. By approximately 1760, the piano began rivaling the harpsichord as the most popular keyboard instrument.

Pitch and the Hertz

Today a unit of measuring called hertz is used to determine how high or low a note is. Hertz measures the frequency of sound waves. Modern orchestras tune to an A note set at 440 hertz. Before the hertz measurement, an A note could be higher or lower from instrument to instrument or place to place. Existing baroque instruments reveal pitches were lower during the baroque period. An A note in Bach's time was 415 hertz, lower than our modern A note. The 440 hertz setting for A was decided by international agreement in the 1930s.

One reason for the piano's rising popularity is that, unlike the harpsichord, a piano allows for dynamics. A piano is played by pushing a key that hits the strings with a small hammer. The harder the pianist hits the key, the louder the sound. With the piano, keyboardists finally had a way to control the volume of their playing.

Public Concerts

First produced in 1597, opera grew during the baroque period. With its blend of drama, music, and dance, opera was an exciting new kind of musical performance. It was ornate and dramatic, qualities people valued during the baroque era. Beginning in Venice, Italy, opera slowly spread throughout Italy and eventually Europe. The growing popularity of opera also led to the rise of public opera houses and concert halls. In 1638, the first public opera house was built in Venice. No longer were elaborate musical productions only for the nobility. In 1680, the first public concert hall was built in London. Opera houses and concert halls were built all across Europe, and they featured talented soloists.

Similar to today, concert tickets were expensive, so most concertgoers were well-to-do. Less expensive music making took place informally, at home and at

Baroque opera houses were very elaborately decorated.

work, among friends and family. Many songs, dances, and folk remained part of the unwritten history of music at the time.

Chapter 5

A Shift to Lighter Music

In some ways, the relationship between artistic movements is like the pendulum of a clock. Attitudes and views swing one way. Then with time, they swing back. Near the end of the baroque period, some people thought music was too elaborate and artificial. People were tired of complicated dissonance and fancy flourishes. They wanted a new, simpler style with pleasant melodies. Composers began writing more songlike music, in which the melodies stood out with light accompaniment underneath. This homophonic style also used fewer chords. It had little or no dissonance.

Classical composers created orchestra symphonies, in which the conductor leads the orchestra into four different movements.

Classical and Orderly

This era became known as the classical period. The classical period was approximately 1750 to 1830 CE. Classical composers sought to create music that had a clear logic and structure. Similar to the simple, classic lines of an ancient Greek temple, composers wanted music that was balanced, beautiful, and orderly.

Classical composers were not the only ones who appreciated reason and order. The classical period occurred during a time called the Enlightenment. Also called the Age of Reason, the Enlightenment was led by French philosophers such as Voltaire, Rousseau, and Montesquieu. These leaders believed in the power of logical thinking and reason. They believed humans could understand and improve the world through clear thinking. This enlightened view valued reason more than the power of the church or monarchs. In the United States, Enlightenment values influenced leaders such as Thomas Jefferson, Benjamin Franklin, and Thomas Paine.

This was also a time of great political unrest. The American Revolution (1765–1783), French Revolution (1789–1799), and the Napoleonic Wars (1803–1815) all helped shape the classical period. In America, British colonists revolted against King George III and laws and taxes the colonists thought were unfair. In France, people rebelled against the disastrous economic policies of the French monarchy. After the French Revolution, Napoléon Bonaparte took control of the French army and conquered most of Europe, until he too was defeated in 1815. As revolutionaries called for liberty and equality, people rejected the rule of monarchs and the nobility. The nobility became less influential. Musicians could no longer count on the support of wealthy patrons. More and more, musicians had to rely on a public audience willing to pay for music. The careers of classical composers reflect these gradual shifts.

Sonata Form

The sonata form was very popular during the classical period. The sonata is a musical composition with an A part, a B part, then another A part. The first A part is called the exposition. This part exposes all the musical ingredients the composer is going to use. The B part is called the development. This part develops, or reworks, the material from the exposition. The last A part is called the recapitulation. This part repeats the exposition but with some changes. In part owing to the ability of listeners to recognize the return of the original theme in the recapitulation, the sonata was the most popular musical form of the classical period.

Three of the best-known composers of the classical period are Franz Joseph Haydn (1732–1809), Wolfgang Amadeus Mozart (1756–1791), and Ludwig van Beethoven (1770–1827). Because all three lived in Vienna, Austria, they were called the Viennese School. Haydn, Mozart, and Beethoven knew each other. Haydn and Mozart were even friends.

Franz Joseph Haydn Creates an Extended Tune

Both Haydn and Mozart showed musical talent at a very young age. Haydn was five years old when his musical talent was discovered. At age eight, he was sent to Vienna to sing as a choirboy. But once Haydn's voice broke, the choir no longer wanted him. By age 17, he was living in poverty as a music teacher. He eventually became the accompanist and servant to an Italian composer. In 1761, a Hungarian prince hired Haydn, and he worked for this royal family for 30 years. As court composer, Haydn was expected to write and

> After his burial, Haydn's skull was stolen. It was not returned until the 1950s.

Haydn is also sometimes called the father of the string quartet, in part because he created a standard quartet form.

conduct music, supervise the court orchestra, arrange and direct opera music, play for small chamber groups, and write many types of music to please his patron.

Haydn developed musical themes through an extended tune. This extended tune changed in the second half of a piece, creating a classical and pleasant-sounding whole.

Wolfgang Amadeus Mozart Incorporates Different Musical Styles

Unlike Haydn, Mozart never had steady funding from an aristocratic patron. As a result, Mozart often faced serious financial worries throughout his life. Like his friend Haydn, Mozart's talent was discovered early. He was truly a child of stunning musical talent. He played the harpsichord at age three and composed his first music at age five. Mozart's father was a talented violinist himself. Mozart's sister Maria Anna also played the keyboard brilliantly, so Mozart's father took his talented children on tour.

One man described giving eight-year-old Mozart some original music. The man had brought the music with him because he wanted to be certain Mozart had never seen the music before. Mozart sat at the keyboard and immediately began playing the piece perfectly, not only with correct notes but with correct speed and style, something many adult musicians could not do.

Unfortunately, like other childhood stars, Mozart discovered he was not as popular once he grew up. He struggled financially and, unlike Haydn, was unable to secure a steady court position until the last few years of his life. Nevertheless, his music is considered some of the greatest ever written. As one critic put it, "Mozart *is* music."[1]

Today, Mozart's talent of incorporating different styles of music would be a bit like a rock musician who

As a child, Mozart traveled throughout Europe with his father and sister, playing for nobility.

could also write musicals, country music, classical music, and hip-hop. A good example of Mozart's remarkable ability is in his opera *Don Giovanni*. This opera includes a comic character named Donna Elvira. Elvira is a drama queen who likes to think of herself as a tragic heroine. She has a solo in which she explodes on the cheating romantic male lead, Don Giovanni.

Mozart wrote Elvira's part in a baroque style, a style 50 years old at the time. As a result, Elvira comes across as phony and exaggerated. At another point in the opera, Mozart has three kinds of dance bands onstage at once. Each band is playing a different style of music, yet Mozart masterfully coordinates all three. Mozart's talent set a standard for excellence few other composers have attained.

Beethoven's Experimental Style

The final composer of the Viennese School is Beethoven. For a time, Beethoven was a student of Haydn, but his stormy personality often made him difficult to work with. He and Haydn soon parted ways. Beethoven's early music is similar to Haydn's and Mozart's but with more drama and flair. This early period of Beethoven's work (to approximately 1802) is the first of three distinct styles in his music.

Beethoven's middle period (1802–1815) is sometimes called heroic because the music he wrote during this time suggests struggle and triumph. Beethoven's Third Symphony, written from 1803–1804, is even subtitled "Eroica," which is Italian for "heroic." While composing his Third Symphony, Beethoven discovered his hearing was worsening.

One of the great tragedies of Beethoven's life was when he became deaf. Although he continued composing even after he was deaf, sound and music were Beethoven's life. Losing his hearing almost drove him to suicide. But instead, Beethoven poured his pain and emotion into his music. As his hearing failed, Beethoven became increasingly withdrawn. Because of his personal challenges, this final stage of his music, his late period (1815–1827), became increasingly experimental. Beethoven's changing style showed a growing emotion and moodiness.

Beethoven's Ninth Symphony

In the classical period, the main work composed for orchestra was the symphony. A symphony usually has four sections called movements: a fast section, a slow section, a calm dance movement, and a faster fourth section. Beethoven's Ninth Symphony was unusual because it also included a chorus of singers. The finale to the Ninth Symphony, called "Ode to Joy," has a special place in world music. It was played during a 1989 Christmas celebration commemorating the fall of the Berlin Wall. It is the official anthem of the European Union countries. In Japan, "Ode to Joy" is often played at New Year's Eve concerts with thousands of choir members.

CLASSICAL
Composers

Franz Joseph Haydn's compositional technique was creating a musical theme and then developing it. He created an extended tune for the first part of the music and then changed this tune for the second half. These two parts were not identical, but because they were similar, they formed a unified and pleasing whole. Haydn was a very productive composer, writing 106 symphonies and 67 pieces for string quartets.

Wolfgang Amadeus Mozart displayed a unique talent for understanding and incorporating different styles of music. A master of all genres, Mozart created music that is bright and brilliant with a thread of sorrow. His operas show not only great drama but also insight into human nature.

Ludwig van Beethoven deeply influenced Western music, particularly with his symphonies. The first four notes of his Fifth Symphony (du-du-du-duuuun) are some of the most famous notes in the world. The finale to his Ninth Symphony, also known as "Ode to Joy," has been broadcast around the world to celebrate the triumph of the human spirit. Beethoven's changing and emotional style straddled the classical period and the romantic musical period that followed.

Chapter 6

Romantic Pianists

$\mathcal{B}$eethoven's changing style reflected a growing emotion and moodiness that was part of the musical period known as romanticism. The word *romantic* refers to a type of story written during the medieval period. A romance told about a noble person doing heroic deeds, such as King Arthur's quest or Sir Gawain's battle with a dragon. The term *romantic* was first used to describe writers and poets of the 1800s such as poet William Wordsworth and novelist Victor Hugo. (Hugo's book *Les Misérables* is also now a popular musical.)

Unlike classical music, romantic music was less concerned with elegant, beautiful form and more concerned with expressing emotion. Although most

The Industrial Revolution allowed for mass-production of many products, including the piano.

music has some romantic elements, music from the romantic period emphasizes creating picturesque images, revealing the composer's feelings and exploring the unknown—including the supernatural and the powers of nature. The romantic period also idealized youthfulness, nature, and peasant life.

In part, the romantic era was a reaction to the Industrial Revolution, a time when machines dramatically changed the economy. The Industrial Revolution began in England with the invention of the steam engine in 1712. Soon new inventions and machines were revolutionizing the way people worked. Items that had been made by hand for centuries, such as cloth, could now be mass-produced in factories. Many people took advantage of these work opportunities. People left their homes in the countryside and moved to cities to work in large factories. Despite the long hours and often terrible working conditions, the Industrial Revolution brought financial success to many. One benefit of the Industrial Revolution was that many

> **Before the Industrial Revolution, the clock and the organ were the most complicated machines built.**

items that had once been costly and time-consuming to make could now be produced more quickly and easily. As the cost of goods dropped, people were now able to buy things that had once been too expensive.

Producing More Pianos

The Industrial Revolution revolutionized the way instruments were made, particularly the piano. Before the Industrial Revolution, every piece of a piano was made by hand. In the 1770s, piano makers could only make approximately 20 pianos per year. By 1800, one piano company was making 400 pianos per year. By 1850, a piano company could build 2,000 pianos per year.[1]

Pianos were suddenly affordable and very popular. Before television, movies, and computers, playing and singing music together was a widespread form of entertainment. As more people became amateur musicians, they wanted more music to play. More instrumental music and songs were produced and sold than ever before. In the 1770s, music publishers offered hundreds of sheet music choices. In the 1820s, they offered tens of thousands. Music publishers paid attention to what their customers wanted. Vocal music

The invention of the steam engine in 1712 sparked the Industrial Revolution and a different way of life in England.

such as the *lied* (German for "song") was popular. The German composer Franz Schubert wrote more than 600 lieder, and home concerts of his songs were called Schubertiads. In addition, hundreds of composers wrote parlor music that was easy for amateur performers to play. Two parlor songs still familiar today are "Oh! Susanna" and "Camptown Races," written by the American composer Stephen Foster.

In addition to the piano music of the time, dance music, particularly the waltz, was popular during the romantic era. The waltz started in Vienna in the late 1800s, and its classic form is called the Viennese Waltz. With its sweeping 1-2-3 beat, the waltz was one of the first dances in which men and women could hold each other. A father and son, both named Johann Strauss, wrote some of the best-known waltzes of the time, including the "Blue Danube Waltz."

Female Musicians

During the 1800s, home music was particularly important for women. Although many working-class women labored in factories, women from wealthier families were expected to stay home. Singing and music lessons kept women and girls busy. Musical talent was considered a lovely skill that could add to home life and attract a husband.

Clara Wieck (1819–1896) and Fanny Mendelssohn (1805–1847) were both professional musicians during the romantic period. Wieck gave her first public piano performance at age nine. By the time she was 20, Wieck was a leading pianist in Europe. Against her father's wishes, she married one of his piano students, the composer Robert Schumann. Clara Schumann performed less after her marriage and the birth of her eight children, but she continued performing,

Clara Schumann taught, performed, and composed music until she died at the age of 77.

composing, and teaching. She also edited her husband's music.

Fanny Mendelssohn was also related to a famous composer. Fanny's younger brother Felix was a child prodigy much like Mozart, and he was very close to his older sister Fanny. Although Fanny too was a talented pianist and composer, her family opposed her playing music professionally. She published some of her music under her brother's name. Fanny's husband was more supportive of her music than her father was, and she published several books of songs and many short piano pieces after she married.

Romantic Composers

More pianos and more amateur pianists meant a need for more music teachers. Many composers, including Frederic Chopin and Franz Liszt, were private piano teachers. Musicians now earned a living mainly by performing, teaching, or composing for the general public. The nobility and the church were less influential, and they were no longer the giant patrons of music they once had been. In the past, a court composer may have needed to play several instruments and write all different types of music. Romantic composers instead specialized in a specific instrument.

For example, the violinist Paganini and pianists Chopin and Liszt were known as virtuosos. Liszt was also the first person to call his performances recitals. So dazzling were Liszt's recitals, there were reports of "Lisztomania" as female fans went crazy at his performances. Liszt played so forcefully pianos broke onstage.

These virtuoso musicians composed music that was complex and challenging to play. Their works were a far cry from the relatively easy parlor music composed for amateur musicians. Romantic composers were also discovering they now had to compete against classic pieces of the past. Prior to the 1780s, people attended concerts expecting to hear new music. Composers were eventually forgotten as people moved on to the next big thing. But now musical classics were emerging, pieces that were performed long after a composer died. Musicians compared themselves to the greats of the past, particularly Beethoven. They also had to compete against this great music of the past. Romantic composers tried developing throughout their own unique styles. They wanted originality that would set them apart.

Romanticism in Music

During the romantic era, new styles of music developed. For example, there were character pieces, also called mood pictures, which were short piano pieces that captured the mood or character of a person or idea. Robert Schumann wrote a character piece called

Kinderszenen (*Scenes from Childhood*) that evoked the simple joys of childhood. For another type of romantic music, Liszt coined the terms *programme music* and *symphonic poem*. These were exclusively instrumental pieces that told a story from literature, mythology, or history.

Another romantic composer, the German composer Richard Wagner, composed many operas based on Norse and Germanic mythology. His most famous opera, *Der Ring des Nibelungen*, often called the *Ring* cycle, is a series of four separate operas performed over four days, totaling approximately 20 hours. Wagner's music is well-known for using leitmotifs. Leitmotifs are short musical themes that represent a person or idea and reappear throughout the music. Darth Vader's theme in the Star Wars movies is an example of a leitmotif.

WAITING FOR TICKETS
Performances of Wagner's *Ring* cycle at the Bayreuth, Germany, opera house are so popular there is a waiting list for tickets. It can take as long as 10 years to get tickets.[2] It took Wagner even longer to compose the *Ring* cycle: 26 years.

While Wagner produced his dramatic German opera, opera was also flowering in France and Italy. In Italy in particular, opera was very popular. In fact, in 1825, if asked to name the most famous composer alive,

NATIONALISM IN MUSIC

One emotion that appealed to romantic composers was patriotism. During the romantic period, many romantic composers were interested in nationalism, music that reflected their homeland or nationality. Some, such as Liszt, wrote music based on the folk songs and dances of their native country. Others, such as Wagner, wrote music that connected to a story or legend from their nation. Still others, such as American conductor John Philip Sousa, wrote music to spur patriotic feelings. In 1897, Sousa composed "The Stars and Stripes Forever," a band march that is performed regularly during patriotic American events such as the Fourth of July.

most people would not have said Beethoven. They would have said Rossini, an Italian composer famous for his operas. Two of Rossini's well-known operas are *Il Barbiere di Siviglia* (*The Barber of Seville*) and *Guillame Tell* (*William Tell*). Opera was so popular many people attended four or five times a week. Opera houses were built to entertain. Besides a stage and concert hall, opera houses often contained restaurants, casinos, and public areas for socializing. Italian composers Giuseppe Verdi and Giacomo Puccini also wrote operas that are still famous.

In opera, emotion and drama are created through music. Many of the expressive techniques used in opera are also used in film, television, and video game music. Near the end of the romantic period, Verdi's operas were still drawing wide audiences. But a gap was developing between art music and popular music.

Art music and popular music had been the same in the past. Mozart appealed to the musical elite and the general public. So did Verdi. But Wagner's epic opera was too somber and serious for some people. People wanted music that was fun and entertaining. People would soon have more musical choices than ever before, thanks to the technology of the 1900s.

Concert Customs and Etiquette

Some of the customs audiences take part in today were introduced by romantic composers. As conductor of the Vienna State Opera House (1897–1907), composer Gustav Mahler insisted no one clap between movements of a musical composition. Audiences still follow this rule today.

Modern audiences are also accustomed to dimming the lights before a performance, an innovation introduced by Wagner. The first time Wagner held a full performance of his *Ring* cycle, he dimmed the lights in the area where the audience was sitting. It was so unexpected the audience gasped.

Chapter 7

A Time of Change

The 1900s were a time of tremendous change, both for the world and for music. On June 28, 1914, a Serbian rebel assassinated Archduke Ferdinand of Austria-Hungary and his wife, sparking World War I (1914–1918). Nations took sides until eventually most of Europe had entered the war, along with other countries worldwide. The two sides were called the Allies (including the United Kingdom, France, Russia, Italy, Japan, and the United States) and the Central powers (including Germany, Austria-Hungary, the Ottoman Empire, and Bulgaria). The war ended on November 11, 1918, with the defeat of the Central powers.

Advances in technologies in the early 1900s, including the gramophone, allowed people to listen to music in their homes.

World War I challenged people's faith in human progress. During the Industrial Revolution, people had taken great pride in progress. Human ingenuity seemed to be making the world better and better. People thought advances would continue indefinitely.

World War I destroyed this illusion. People discovered the machines that had improved life so dramatically could also be used to destroy it. Inventions such as poison gas, machine guns, tanks, and airplanes completely changed how wars were fought. People were killed in ways and in huge numbers never before imagined.

World War I then planted the seeds of the next great war, World War II (1939–1945). After World War I, peace treaties were signed. The Versailles Treaty demanded harsh punishment for Germany. The harsh terms of the Versailles treaty influenced Adolf Hitler and led to World War II.

THE GREAT DEPRESSION

Although the early 1920s was a time of economic prosperity for the United States, in October 1929, the US economy collapsed. The country was thrown into the worst economic period in its history, known as the Great Depression. By 1932, roughly one-third of Americans were out of work.[1] The Depression was a time of tremendous hardship and suffering. Many artists of this time wanted to create works that related to the concerns of the common man, the average worker who struggled against the economic and social problems of the day. Blues, country, and other popular music also reflected these concerns.

In January 1933, Hitler became chancellor of Germany. He promised to make Germany great once again. In 1936, German forces began taking territory. In 1939, Hitler invaded Czechoslovakia and got ready to attack Poland. Great Britain and France promised to aid Poland if it was attacked. On September 1, 1939, German forces invaded Poland. Two days later, France and Great Britain declared war. World War II had begun. The United States joined the Allies on December 8, 1941, after the Japanese attacked Pearl Harbor the day before. World War II ended on September 2, 1945. World War II was the largest and bloodiest war in history, with 40 to 50 million deaths.[2]

During these times of crisis, music provided a way to express patriotism, heartache, and hope. Songs such as "It's a Long Way to Tipperary" and "I'll be Home for Christmas" reflected soldiers longing for home. Some music was dissonant and stark, reflecting the harshness of modern life. Music also offered a break from the realities of life. The swing music of World War II included a 1939 song by the Benny Goodman Sextet called "Seven Come Eleven." Featured on this recording was a brand new instrument that would soon rock the world: the electric guitar.

By the early 1920s, 10 million US households owned radios.

During the 1900s, the gap between art music and popular music grew. Modern technology sped up this process. Recording technology, such as the gramophone, radio, and record player, gave people many more choices about what to listen to and when to listen to it. People had more freedom than ever in selecting music. They could hear music from around the world, music they may have never discovered otherwise.

Radio broadcasters first used the term *classical music* in the 1930s when radio stations created new labels to identify the kind of music they aired. During the 1900s, classical music largely went in two directions. First, as had been done during the romantic era, classical music looked to the past. At classical concerts, audiences expected and wanted to hear music that had been written long before by great composers of the past, such as Beethoven and Bach. Second, the classical musical being written was becoming increasingly experimental and dissonant.

The Rising Dissonance

Composers were still creating pieces with harmony and consonance. But as the romantic era ended, composers began using dissonance in new ways. For example, French composer Debussy and the German composer Mahler used chromaticism. To understand chromaticism, think about a piano keyboard. The piano has both black and white keys. Chromatic tones are created by moving up or down a keyboard from black key to white key to black key and so on. One of Mahler's admirers, Arnold Shoenberg, took this trend even further. After writing atonal music, Schoenberg then developed what he called the 12-tone system. Called serialism, this system uses a series of 12 notes. The notes are put in a random order and then must be used in that order by the composer. Melody and consonance are not central to the music.

Trained musicians were almost the only people who could appreciate this challenging type of music. To the average listener, much of it sounded like noise instead of music. Some music experts did not like it either. German composer Otto Taubmann said, "If this is the music of the future, then I pray my Creator not to let me live to hear it again."[3]

Jazz and Its Relatives

Twentieth-century listeners had many musical choices. They could change the radio station or put on a record and listen to something else. In 1921, 100 million records were sold, compared with only 27 million records in 1914.[5] In 1922, 10 million US

The Fisk Jubilee Singers

The Fisk Jubilee Singers were an African-American choir from Fisk University in Tennessee. Their parents had been slaves, and the Jubilee Singers sang spirituals as part of their concerts. In 1873, they toured Great Britain as part of a fund-raising program for their university. They performed for Queen Victoria and other royalty. They also gave a concert at the prime minister's home and were personally invited by the prime minister to a private meal with his family. Successfully touring for an entire year, the Jubilee Singers raised nearly $1 million for their university.[4]

households owned radios, up from just 60,000 in 1919.[6]

Some of the most popular kinds of music playing on the radio in the early 1900s were blues, ragtime, swing, and jazz. These types of music have African-American roots. When African slaves were first brought to America in the 1700s, they developed their own distinctive music. They created songs called spirituals, which combined African songs with hymns. The tunes and lyrics of spirituals reflected the pain and injustice African Americans experienced and their hopes for deliverance.

Blues uses sad melodies to tell about the sorrows of life, such as poverty, hunger, injustice, and lost love. Two of the great female blues singers were Bessie Smith and Billie Holiday. Ragtime music developed from African-American dance styles. The most famous ragtime composer of his day was Scott Joplin.

BILLIE HOLIDAY'S "STRANGE FRUIT"

One of Billie Holiday's most famous songs is "Strange Fruit," a song about racism. She first sang this blues song in 1939, long before the civil rights movement. The civil rights movement, which began in the 1960s, fought to end the unfair treatment of African Americans in the United States. The lyrics to "Strange Fruit" come from a poem written by Abel Meeropol, a white Jewish man who was disturbed by racism. Even though some people opposed her, Billie Holiday boldly sang "Strange Fruit," and millions heard her song.

His songs "The Entertainer" and "Maple Leaf Rag" are two well-known ragtime tunes.

As blues, ragtime, and dance music mixed, jazz was born. Jazz first appeared in the 1910s. New Orleans has been called the "cradle of jazz."[7] And one of the most famous jazz performers to come from New Orleans was Louis Armstrong (1901–1971).

Louis Armstrong Masters Improvisation

As a child, Armstrong lived in one of New Orleans's toughest and poorest neighborhoods. From a young age, Armstrong worked odd jobs to help put food on the table. At age 11, he had to drop out of school to help

Armstrong quite possibly influenced jazz more than any other musician.

support his family. Then a Jewish family Armstrong had worked for took him in. The Karnofsky family helped feed, clothe, and house Armstrong. They loaned him money to buy his first instrument: a cornet, similar to a trumpet. He never forgot their

> Jazz musician Louis Armstrong was nicknamed "satchelmouth" because his cheeks blew up so big when he played the cornet.

generosity. In their honor, as an adult Armstrong wore a Star of David pendant, a symbol of the Jewish faith.

Eventually Armstrong moved to Chicago, Illinois. He changed from the cornet to the trumpet, and his career took off. Armstrong was particularly good at improvisation. When musicians improvise they do not use written or memorized music. Improvisation is a standard jazz technique, and Armstrong was a master. His trumpet solos helped make solos an integral part of jazz performance.

Other Jazz Stars

Armstrong was also one of the jazz musicians who developed scat singing. Scat singing means to insert nonsense words and syllables into a song instead of actual words. For example, a singer might sing, "shoo be do" or "be bop." Another great jazz performer who included scat singing was Ella Fitzgerald.

Many jazz musicians became celebrities. Many, such as Armstrong, had risen from poverty. Many were also African American. Despite their fame and talent, many African-American musicians endured unfair treatment. There was widespread racism at the time, particularly in the southern United States. Voting laws unfairly limited African Americans' right to vote. Segregation laws created unfair treatment of African Americans. For example, African Americans could not attend white schools, could not enter white libraries, and could not drink from "whites only" drinking fountains. Many African-American musicians worked to end these unfair practices. For example, singer Nat King Cole refused to sing in segregated nightclubs and concert halls that had been divided into "white only" and "black only" areas.

While recording "Mack the Knife," jazz singer Ella Fitzgerald started scat singing because she had forgotten the words.

George Gershwin's Jazz Concerto

Rhapsody in Blue, written by American composer George Gershwin, is a masterful blend of jazz and classical music. Composed in just five weeks, *Rhapsody in Blue* is a one-movement jazz concerto for solo piano and jazz ensemble. *Rhapsody in Blue* was originally written for a 1924 concert in New York called *An Experiment in Modern Music*. The goal of the concert, and its conductor Paul Whiteman, was to encourage classical music lovers to appreciate jazz and to get jazz lovers to try classical music. Gershwin considered jazz "an American folk music" that was "in the blood and feeling of the American people."[8] Apparently, Gershwin was right. His 14-minute-long *Rhapsody in Blue* was a hit. The audience loved it. Although critics initially belittled it, when Gershwin recorded the concerto in 1927, it quickly sold 1 million copies.[9]

Movies and Musicals

Movies and movie music became important phenomena in the 1900s. The earliest movies were silent films. Realizing music would add to the drama onscreen, theaters added live music. Depending on the size of the theater, a pianist, organist, or orchestra played music that matched the action onscreen. Eventually recorded soundtracks replaced live movie music. The first film with a recorded soundtrack was the 1926 film *Don Juan*. Today, classical music thrives in film. Soundtracks from movies such as *Finding Nemo* and the Chronicles of Narnia and Harry Potter series all feature classical music by talented modern composers. Classical movie

Film Music

Movies use music in several ways. Source music, which is also called diegetic music, is music heard or played by the characters in the film. If the main character in the movie sits down and plays the piano, this is source music. Underscoring, or nondiegetic music, is music characters cannot hear. If the main character is walking through a dark forest at night, the spooky music the audience hears is underscoring. If the underscoring sounded like gentle, peaceful music, it would create a very different feeling for the audience. Underscoring is extremely important in creating the mood of a movie. A great example of this is the music that accompanies the shark in the movie *Jaws*.

music is quite popular. In fact, movie music is regularly performed by symphony orchestras.

Hollywood also made movies that featured another new type of twentieth-century performance—the musical. Some well-known musicals are *Oklahoma*, *The Sound of Music*, *West Side Story*, and *Annie*. Combining drama, music, and dance, musicals are an American invention. They are related to opera and vaudeville, a type of musical variety show popular in the early 1900s. Today, many musicals are spin-offs of popular books and movies, such as *Wicked* and *Shrek the Musical*.

ALL KINDS OF MUSICALS

There are many different types of musicals:

- Jukebox – A musical based on pop or rock music. For example, *Mamma Mia* is based on the music of pop group ABBA.
- Book – A musical with a clear plot, not necessarily based on a book. *The Sound of Music* is a book musical.
- Movie/Television Adaptation – A musical based on a movie or television show such as *Shrek the Musical*.
- Operatic – A musical in which all words are sung. There is no spoken dialogue. *The Phantom of the Opera* is an operatic musical.
- Revue – A musical without a story line or plot. A revue, such as *Side by Side by Sondheim*, showcases songs.

Chapter 8

The Rise of Rock 'n' Roll

World War II ended in 1945, but it was many years before Europe recovered from the war's devastating effects. Meanwhile, US financial and industrial strength had actually increased as a result of the war effort. The United States was now a dominant world power.

American music was also dominating the music scene—particularly a crazy new music called rock 'n' roll. In 1951 a Cleveland, Ohio, disc jockey named Alan Freed invented the term *rock 'n' roll* to describe the albums he was playing on his radio station. He also organized the Moondog Coronation Ball in 1952, now considered the very first rock concert.

Elvis Presley, the King of Rock 'n' Roll, was one of the biggest cultural icons of the mid to late 1900s.

Chuck Berry was known for playing guitar while doing his famous duck walk.

Two great performers during rock's early days were Little Richard and Chuck Berry. Chuck Berry became one of the first African-American performers with a major pop hit, "Maybellene."

As a new style of music, rock 'n' roll developed from jazz (particularly the blues), country music, and popular songs. From rhythm and blues, rock music got its pounding 1-2-3-4 beat. Commonly referred to as the backbeat, the emphasis was placed on counts 2 and 4 rather than 1 and 3. From country, rock inherited guitar as the background instrument. Rock musicians especially loved the electric guitar, which had been invented in 1931.

Rock 'n' Roll Superstars

The early rock 'n' rollers were soon overshadowed by rock 'n' roll's first superstar: Elvis Presley. Presley had been raised in the South on the music of country and gospel, and his singing reflected these styles. He was known for a crooning, yearning tone in his voice. His swiveling hips caused quite a ruckus, and parents protested his shocking performance singing "Hound Dog" on the 1956 television program

THE BIRTH OF COUNTRY MUSIC

Between World War I and World War II, country music spread through radio shows and recordings. Country music was influenced by many types of music: folk ballads, cowboy songs, popular songs of the 1800s and 1900s, blues, gospel, and banjo music. Country developed in several styles, including western swing, honky-tonk, and bluegrass. Today a number of country artists are crossover artists, which means they are popular with a wide variety of listeners. Taylor Swift is a crossover artist who is popular not only with country music lovers but with people who listen to pop music, too.

The Milton Berle Show. Teens loved his smooth voice and wild dancing. Elvis is nicknamed the King of Rock 'n' Roll for good reason. Of all rock musicians, he holds the record for most Top 10 hits, most Top 40 hits, and most weeks at number one on the charts.

By 1960, rock music had spread worldwide. It was outselling every other kind of music. The booming economy after World War II gave many families—and particularly teenagers—more spending money. Kids had their own radios and their own record players. They were buying their own music. For the first time, record companies began selling music produced specifically for teens: pop music.

In 1963, the Beatles rose to the top. Beatlemania first spread through Great Britain. When the Fab Four toured the United States in 1964, the Beatles began what came to be called the British Invasion of rock bands. Like Franz Liszt during the romantic period, the Beatles also had hysterical female fans, and by 1966, the Beatles decided to stop touring. They focused instead on producing albums in a music studio.

The Beatles were very musically innovative. They added unusual instruments to their songs, such as the harpsichord and an Indian harp called a *svaramandal*.

The Beatles performed on the *Ed Sullivan Show* on February 9, 1964.

They included musical styles from past eras such as the music hall sound of "When I'm Sixty-Four," the double string quartet of "Eleanor Rigby," and the brass band in "Sergeant Pepper's Lonely Hearts Club Band." The Beatles's experimentation with different styles of music and different instruments helped keep people interested in these older types of music.

GIRL GROUPS AND BOY BANDS

Boy bands and girl groups have been popular throughout the history of rock 'n' roll. These groups were bands with all female or all male performers in their late teens or early twenties. Some of the early girl groups were the Shirelles, the Marvelettes, and the Ronettes. The Ronettes toured with the Beatles. More recent girl and boy groups include Icona Pop and One Direction. Sometimes band members are family as well, such as the Jackson 5 and the Osmond Brothers.

Rock Splinters

As rock music grew, it began splintering into many different styles. There was folk rock of the 1960s and 1970s. There was the Motown sound created by soul musicians such as Marvin Gaye and Stevie Wonder. There was surfer rock including the Beach Boys, Latino rock such as Tex-Mex, and salsa. There was disco, punk, funk, hip-hop, rap, and many more types.

The folk music of the 1960s and 1970s was in part a reaction against rock and its electronic technology, electric guitars, and synthesizers. Folk musicians looked back to traditional songs and traditional ways of performing music. This attitude carried into classical music as well in a movement called "early music." Early music sought to reproduce classical music using the original instruments and performance styles of earlier eras. Another goal of early music was rediscovering little-known classical pieces.

Classical music was changing in others ways as well. Traditional classical music could still be found in concert halls as well as in orchestra and band classes in schools. But modern classical composers did not want traditional music. They wanted to experiment with sound and tones. By the early 1950s, many classical composers had adopted the composer Schoenberg's 12-tone system. The composer John Cage developed the prepared piano in 1938. To play his prepared piano, Cage took random objects, such as screws, bolts, plastic, pieces of wood, rubber, and more, and put them in between the piano strings. This practice made the piano sound more like a drum or other percussion instrument.

Cage also experimented with aleatory music, also called chance music because much of the composition was left up to chance. Cage's piece "Imaginary Landscape No. 4" required 12 radios, 24 players, and one conductor. The conductor directed the rhythm and dynamics, but the players chose which radio stations

John Cage believed any sound could be considered music. In 1984, he recorded a live performance of himself playing an amplified cactus with a feather.

Cage enjoyed experimenting with different sounds, even if it meant listeners did not understand his style.

they played, when to start playing, and other factors that were left to chance. Cage liked to ask the question, "What is music?" According to Cage, "Everything we do is music."[1]

Still other composers, such as Steve Reich, were interested in minimalism and phasing. Minimalism uses simple, short melodies and chords that are repeated over and over. This music can have a hypnotic feel to it. Phasing is music that changes so gradually for such a long period of time that it is hard to notice the changes. Reich described these repetitive patterns as a form of meditation. Reich also experimented with sampling.

Classical and popular composers experimented with the new musical world of electronic sound. This mixing of all kinds of music in all kinds of ways is common throughout the entire post–World War II period. And music today is more diverse than ever and yet even more linked. All these different kinds of music give people more ways to express themselves. The history of music has always been one of change. The pendulum of music still swings back and forth today. But today we can learn, play, hear, and create music in more ways than ever before.

> **THE REVOLUTIONARY FOUR MINUTES, 33 SECONDS**
> In 1952, Cage composed his most famous piece of music, "4'33."" Of all of Cage's experimental works, this piece is the most experimental of them all. The "music" directs that performers sit silently at their instruments for four minutes and 33 seconds. There is only silence. All the random noises in the room can be heard as well, such as coughs and the air conditioning. These sounds, according to Cage, are also music.

TIMELINE

43,000 BCE
The oldest known flutes are made.

500 BCE
Pythagoras, Greek philosopher and mathematician, dies. Pythagoras discovered the relationship between music and math.

1000s CE
Guido of Arezzo invents the standard notation system and suggests arranging notes on lines.

Early 1400s
John Dunstable popularizes the chord combination known as the third, which forms the basis of most Western music.

1400s–1600s
The Renaissance period, or period of rebirth, is characterized by a rediscovery of ancient learning and a remarkable blossoming of the arts.

1501
Ottaviano Petrucci publishes the first book of printed music.

1685
Composers Johann Sebastian Bach and George Frideric Handel are born in Germany.

1700
The modern piano is invented.

1732
Classical composer Franz Joseph Haydn is born. He goes on to be called the father of the string quartet because he created a standard quartet form.

1750–1830
The classical period lasts fewer than 100 years.

TIMELINE CONTINUED

1756
Wolfgang Amadeus Mozart is born. He goes on to become one of the greatest composers ever.

1770
Ludwig van Beethoven is born. He gradually becomes deaf but continues to compose despite his disability.

1873
The Jubilee Singers perform in Great Britain, helping raise nearly $1 million for their school.

1876
The microphone is invented.

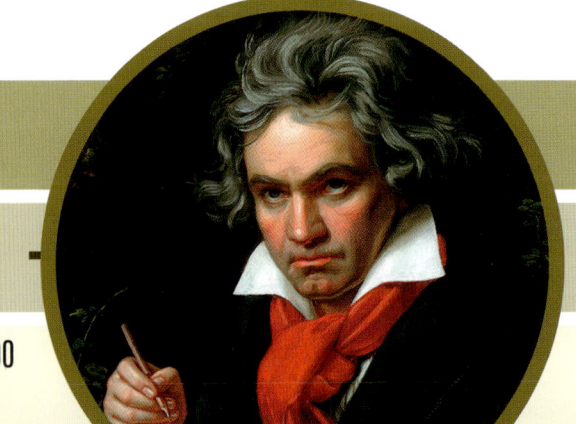

1901
Louis Armstrong is born and lives on to become arguably the greatest jazz performer who ever lived.

1931
The electric guitar is invented.

1951
Disc jockey Alan Freed coins the term *rock 'n' roll*.

1964
The British Invasion begins as the Beatles tour the United States.

GLOSSARY

atonal music
Music without a harmony as a primary element.

concerto
A musical form featuring a solo instrument in the lead role with other instruments accompanying.

consonant
In agreement. Harmonious.

dissonant
Harsh in tone of sound. Not harmonious.

dynamics
How loudly or softly music is played.

homophonic
Music in which one main melody line is supported by chords or other musical material.

improvise
To invent music on the spot and play whatever one feels.

movement
A distinct section of a musical composition. A movement has its own beginning, middle, and end and is part of the larger composition.

oratorio
A religious version of an opera.

pitch
A note is a single pitch. Sometimes the words *pitch* and *note* are used interchangeably.

polyphony
Music that has two or more melodies of equal importance that are sung together.

pop music
Popular music; commercially public music intended for a wide audience.

sampling
Music that takes a piece of recorded sound, chops it into pieces, and then inserts it back into the music in some way.

score
The printed version of a musical composition.

symphony
A musical structure for orchestra, usually with four movements: fast, slow, gentle dance, faster.

synthesizer
An electronic instrument that creates a variety of electronic sounds.

virtuoso
A masterful musician of unusual skill and talent.

ADDITIONAL RESOURCES

Selected Bibliography
Bonds, Mark Evans. *A History of Music in Western Culture*. 2nd ed. Upper Saddle River, NJ: Pearson, 2006. Print.

Burkholder, J. Peter, Donald Jay Grout, and Claude V. Palisca. *A History of Western Music*. 7th ed. New York: W. W. Norton, 2006. Print.

Goodall, Howard. *The Story of Music: From Babylon to the Beatles*. New York: Pegasus, 2013. Print.

Further Readings
Anderson, Jennifer Joline. *John Lennon: Legendary Musician & Beatle*. Minneapolis, MN: Abdo, 2010. Print.

Marsico, Katie. *How to Analyze the Works of Andrew Lloyd Webber*. Minneapolis, MN: Abdo, 2011. Print.

Robertson, Robbie, et al. *Legends, Icons & Rebels: Music that Changed the World*. Plattsburg, NY: Tundra, 2013. Print.

Witmer, Scott. *Songwriting*. Minneapolis, MN: Abdo, 2011. Print.

Websites
To learn more about Essential Library of Cultural History, visit **booklinks.abdopublishing.com**. These links are routinely monitored and updated to provide the most current information available.

Places to Visit
American Jazz Museum
1616 East Eighteenth Street
Kansas City, MO 64108
816-474-8463
http://www.americanjazzmuseum.org
The American Jazz Museum showcases the sights and sounds of jazz through interactive exhibits, films, a jazz club, and a theater.

Rock and Roll Hall of Fame & Museum
1100 Rock and Roll Boulevard
Cleveland, Ohio 44114
216-781-7625
http://www.rockhall.com
The Rock and Roll Hall of Fame & Museum educates visitors, fans, and scholars from around the world about the history and continuing significance of rock 'n' roll music. Its world-class museum collects, preserves, exhibits, and interprets rock 'n' roll.

SOURCE NOTES

Chapter 1. The Explosion of Music

1. Phil Hardy. "Enrico Caruso." *The Faber Companion to 20th Century Popular Music.* Faber and Faber, 2001. Web. 6 June 2014.

2. Mark Evans Bonds. *A History of Music in Western Culture.* 2nd ed. Upper Saddle River, NJ: Pearson, 2006. Print. 538.

Chapter 2. Ancient Influences

None.

Chapter 3. The Rise of the Renaissance

1. Mark Evans Bonds. *A History of Music in Western Culture.* 2nd ed. Upper Saddle River, NJ: Pearson, 2006. Print. 108.

2. Ibid. 171.

3. Howard Goodall. *The Story of Music: From Babylon to the Beatles.* New York: Pegasus, 2013. Print. 53.

Chapter 4. Spectacular Sounds

1. Denis Arnold and Basil Smallman. "Bach." *The Oxford Companion to Music*. Ed. Alison Latham. 1st rev. ed. Oxford: Oxford UP, 2011. E-book. 12 June 2014.
2. "Bach, Johann Sebastian." *The Concise Oxford Dictionary of Music*. Eds. Michael Kennedy and Joyce Bourne Kennedy. 5th ed. Oxford: Oxford UP, 2007. E-book. 12 June 2014.
3. Howard Goodall. *The Story of Music: From Babylon to the Beatles*. New York: Pegasus, 2013. Print. 107.
4. Ibid. 80.
5. Mark Evans Bonds. *A History of Music in Western Culture*. 2nd ed. Upper Saddle River, NJ: Pearson, 2006. Print. 279.

Chapter 5. A Shift to Lighter Music

1. "Mozart, Wolfgang Amadeus." *The Oxford Dictionary of Music*. Eds. Tim Rutherford-Johnson, Michael Kennedy, and Joyce Bourne Kennedy. 6th ed. Oxford: Oxford UP, 2012. E-book. 22 May 2014.

SOURCE NOTES CONTINUED

Chapter 6. Romantic Pianists

1. J. Peter Burkholder, Donald Jay Grout, and Claude V. Palisca. *A History of Western Music*. 7th ed. New York: W. W. Norton and Co., 2006. Print. 600.

2. Jaren S. Hinckley. *The Educated Listener: A New Approach to Music Appreciation*. San Diego, CA: Cognella Academic Publishing, 2014. Print. 144.

Chapter 7. A Time of Change

1. Mark Evans Bonds. *A History of Music in Western Culture*. 2nd ed. Upper Saddle River, NJ: Pearson, 2006. Print. 514.

2. "Causes of World War II." *World History Encyclopedia*. Ed. Alfred J. Andrea and Carolyn Neel. Vol. 18. Santa Barbara, CA: ABC-CLIO, 2011. 520–523. *ABC-CLIO*. Web. 26 June 2014.

3. Mark Evans Bonds. *A History of Music in Western Culture*. 2nd ed. Upper Saddle River, NJ: Pearson, 2006. Print. 580.

4. Howard Goodall. *The Story of Music: From Babylon to the Beatles.* New York: Pegasus, 2013. Print. 240–241.

5. Ibid. 254.

6. Ibid. 249.

7. J. Peter Burkholder, Donald Jay Grout, and Claude V. Palisca. *A History of Western Music.* 7th ed. New York: W. W. Norton and Co., 2006. Print. 769.

8. Mark Evans Bonds. *A History of Music in Western Culture.* 2nd ed. Upper Saddle River, NJ: Pearson, 2006. Print. 569.

9. Howard Goodall. *The Story of Music: From Babylon to the Beatles.* New York: Pegasus, 2013. Print. 253.

Chapter 8. The Rise of Rock 'n' Roll

1. J. Peter Burkholder, Donald Jay Grout, and Claude V. Palisca. *A History of Western Music.* 7th ed. New York: W. W. Norton and Co., 2006. Print. 933–934.

INDEX

African-American music, 80, 81, 84, 90
amateur musicians, 30, 65, 66, 69, 70
Amati, Andrea, 32
Amati, Niccoli, 32
American Revolution, 52
Armstrong, Louis, 82–84

Bach, Johan Sebastian, 38–41, 42, 43, 47, 79
background music, 9
barbershop music, 28
baroque music, 36–49, 50, 58
Beach Boys, 94
Beatles, the, 92–93, 94
Beethoven, Ludwig van, 54, 58–59, 61, 62, 70, 72, 79
Berry, Chuck, 90
blues music, 76, 81–82, 91

Cage, John, 95–96, 97
Caruso, Enrico, 6–8, 11
character pieces, 70–71
Chopin, Frederic, 69
chords, 22, 35, 50, 96
Christianity, 17–18, 40
classical music, 57, 62, 78–79, 85, 86–87, 94–95
classical period, 52–54, 59, 60–61
Cole, Nat King, 84
concerto, 45–46, 85
Corelli, Arcangelo, 44–45
counterpoint, 27, 39
country music, 41, 57, 91
Cristofori, Bartolomeo, 47

dance music, 31, 66, 82
de Forest, Lee, 6
Der Ring des Nibelungen, 71
des Prez, Josquin, 29–30
dissonance, 28, 38, 41, 50, 77, 79
Don Giovanni, 57

Dunstable, John, 22
dynamics, 45, 48, 95

electric guitar, 77, 91, 94
Elizabeth I, 26
Enlightenment, 52

female musicians, 67–69, 81, 94
Fisk Jubilee Singers, 80
Fitzgerald, Ella, 84
folk music, 85, 94
Four Seasons, The, 46
Freed, Alan, 88
French Revolution, 52–53

Gaye, Marvin, 94
Gershwin, George, 85
Great Depression, 76
Greeks, 15–17, 26, 27, 30, 40, 52
Gregory I, Pope, 18, 19
Guido of Arezzo, 21
Gutenberg, Johannes, 30

Handel, George Frideric, 38, 41–43
harmony, 19, 28, 79
harpsichord, 38, 45, 47–48, 56, 92
Haydn, Franz Joseph, 54–56, 58, 60
Henry VIII, 26
Hildegard of Bingen, 17
Holiday, Billie, 81
homophony, 35, 50

Industrial Revolution, 64–65, 76

jazz music, 80–84, 85, 91

Liszt, Franz, 69–70, 71, 92
Little Richard, 90
Louis XIV, 43
Lully, Jean-Baptiste, 43–44
Luther, Martin, 32–34

Mahler, Gustav, 73, 79
melody, 19–20, 28–29, 35, 39, 40, 50, 80, 81, 96
Mendelssohn, Fanny, 67–68
Mendelssohn, Felix, 39
Messiah, 42, 43
Middle Ages, 18, 20, 28
monophony, 18, 22
Monteverdi, Claudio, 36
Motown, 94
movie music, 8, 71, 86–87
Mozart, Wolfgang Amadeus, 54, 55–58, 61, 68, 73

Ninth Symphony, 59, 61
notation, 12, 14, 18, 20–21, 30

opera, 6, 11, 36, 40, 41–42, 43, 48, 55, 57–58, 61, 71–73, 87
organs, 15, 16, 47, 64

Paganini, 69
Petrucci, Ottaviano, 30, 31
piano, 23, 47–48, 65–66, 67, 69–70, 79, 85, 86, 95
pitch, 16, 19, 23, 46, 47
plainchant, 18–19, 22, 28
polyphony, 19, 22, 27, 34–35, 39
Presley, Elvis, 91
printed music, 9, 30, 31, 35, 39
programme music, 71
Protestant Reformation, 32–35
public concerts, 48–49
Puccini, Giacomo, 72
Pythagoras, 16–17, 22

radio, 6, 8, 14, 78, 80–81, 88, 91, 92, 95
ragtime, 81–82
recording, 8, 77–78, 84, 91
Reich, Steve, 96–97
Renaissance, 24–35, 36

Rhapsody in Blue, 85
rhythm, 10, 21, 29, 91, 95
rock 'n' roll, 88, 91–92, 94
romanticism, 39, 57, 61, 62, 64–73, 79, 92
Rossini, 72

Schubert, Franz, 66
Schumann, Clara, 67–68
Schumann, Robert, 67, 70
segregation, 84
serialism, 79–80
Shoenberg, Arnold, 79
Silbermann, Gottfried, 47
Smith, Bessie, 81
sonata, 53
Squier, George, 9
St. Matthew Passion, 39, 40
Stradivari, Antonio, 32
"Strange Fruit," 81
Strauss, Johann, 67
swing music, 77, 81, 91
symphonic poem, 71
symphony, 58, 59, 61, 87

technology, 8, 10, 73, 78, 94
tropes, 20
tuning, 46–47

Verdi, Giuseppe, 72–73
Vivaldi, Antonio, 46
vocal music, 8, 20, 42, 65–66

Wagner, Richard, 39, 71–72, 73
waltz, 66–67
Wieck, Clara, 67
Wonder, Stevie, 94
World War I, 74, 76, 91
World War II, 76–77, 88, 91, 92, 97

ABOUT THE AUTHOR

Shannon Baker Moore is a freelance writer and editor who writes for both adults and children. A college writing instructor and writing coach, she is a member of the Society of Children's Book Writers & Illustrators (SCBWI). Author of *The Korean War* (Essential Library of American Wars series) and *King Tut's Tomb* (Digging Up the Past series), Moore blogs about children's books at www.greatbooksforchildren.com. She and her family have lived throughout the United States and currently call Saint Louis, Missouri, home.

780.9 M00
9/16

DATE DUE

LAKE PARK HIGH SCHOOL
ROSELLE, IL 60172

NOV - 2 2021